Drawing Adirondack Wildlife

For kids, parents, classroom teachers, beginning artists, and naturalists.

Sheri Amsel

3rd Edition - Revised
Exploring Nature Educational Resource
www.exploringnature.org

In loving memory of my father,
Dr. Melvyn B. Amsel
1930-1999

**3rd Edition - Revised
2015**

Published by
Exploring Nature Educational Resource
PO Box 84, Elizabethtown, NY 12932
www.exploringnature.org

Copyright © 2001
by Sheri Amsel
Elizabethtown, New York

All rights reserved.
No part of this book may be reproduced without
written permission of the copyright owner.
ISBN 978-0-9741320-6-8

Contents

How to use this drawing guide..................... 2

INSECTS & SPIDERS

Drawing Insects........................... 3
Cricket..................................... 4
Dragonfly.................................. 5
Grasshopper............................... 6
Honeybee.................................. 7
Ladybug Beetle........................... 8
Swallowtail Butterfly.................... 9
Spiders and Webs........................ 10
Garden Spider............................ 11

BIRDS

Drawing Birds............................ 12
American Goldfinch..................... 13
Black-capped Chickadee............... 14
Canada Goose............................ 15
Cardinal................................... 16
Common Loon............................ 17
Common Merganser..................... 18
Great Blue Heron........................ 19
Great Horned Owl....................... 20
Hairy Woodpecker....................... 21
House Sparrow........................... 22
Robin....................................... 23
Ruby-throated Hummingbird.......... 24
Tree Swallow............................. 25

MAMMALS

Drawing Mammals....................... 26
Mammal Taxonomy...................... 27
Carnivore Families...................... 28

Beaver..................................... 29
Black Bear................................ 30
Bobcat..................................... 31
Coyote..................................... 32
Deer Mouse............................... 33
Deer.. 34
Eastern Chipmunk....................... 35
Flying Squirrel........................... 36
Gray Squirrel............................. 37
Long-tailed Weasel..................... 38
Meadow Vole............................. 39
Moose...................................... 40
Mountain Lion............................ 41
Porcupine................................. 42
Raccoon................................... 43
Red Fox................................... 44
Shrew...................................... 45
Snowshoe Hare.......................... 46
Woodchuck............................... 47

AMPHIBIANS & REPTILES

Bullfrog.................................... 48
Red Eft (Newt).......................... 49
Wood Frog................................ 50
Snapping Turtle......................... 51

FISH

Bass.. 52
Trout....................................... 53

TREES & WILDFLOWERS

Leaves..................................... 54
Spring Wildflowers..................... 55

How to use this drawing guide:

Learning how to draw animals can be enhanced by observation and research. Watch it in the wild, at a zoo or online to see how it moves. Look at photographs of it from every angle. Note how it holds its head, the shape of its ears, how its body moves when its running, how it folds its limbs when it lays down. This has the added benefit of enhancing observation skills in general. You may begin to notice details that seemed unimportant before, but now can lend to the realistic nature of your drawing. You may also notice that you are seeing all things in more detail, not just when you draw.

It may also be helpful to look at the scientific classification of an animal to see which common physical characteristics it shares with other animals related to it. I have included a short discussion of mammal taxonomy in this book in the *Drawing Mammals* section. The similarities shown between animal family members may help you to render them more accurately in your drawings.

There is also scientific evidence that supports the concept that when you use motor skills, such as drawing, you develop new neural pathways that helps bolster your long term memory. So while you are drawing animals and learning a bit about them, you will find that knowledge will stay with you for a long time. Drawing skills can help you learn difficult concepts in any field.

To get started, take a blank piece of paper and look at an animal depicted in the book. Draw the first piece shown in black. Then, slowly add the gray lines in the next picture until your drawing is complete. When you get to the last finished picture you can choose to add the details shown there or keep your drawings simple until you gain more skill over time. The more often you draw each animal, the better your drawings will become.

For more animal drawing tips, go to: **www.exploringnature.org**. Have fun!

Sheri Amsel

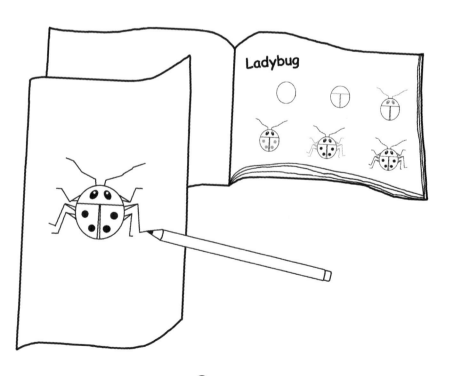

Drawing Insects

Though insects vary in shape and development, in their adult stage they have similar body parts. Every adult insect has three body parts; a head, thorax, and abdomen – though in some, like the ladybug on the opposite page, they may be hidden under the wings. Insects also have six legs, a pair of antennae, and most have two pairs of wings. The legs and wings all originate from the thorax section of the body. Representing this correctly will make your insect drawings look more realistic. Here are some examples below.

Head, thorax, and abdomen starts the rendering of any insect. Watch this turn into the familiar insect shapes that you know.

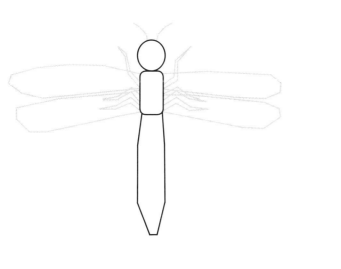

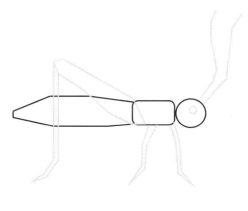

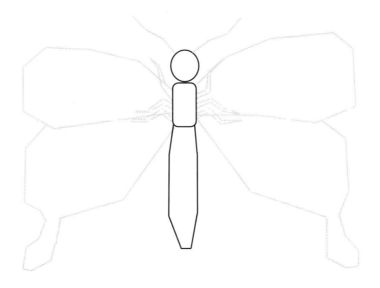

Draw a Cricket

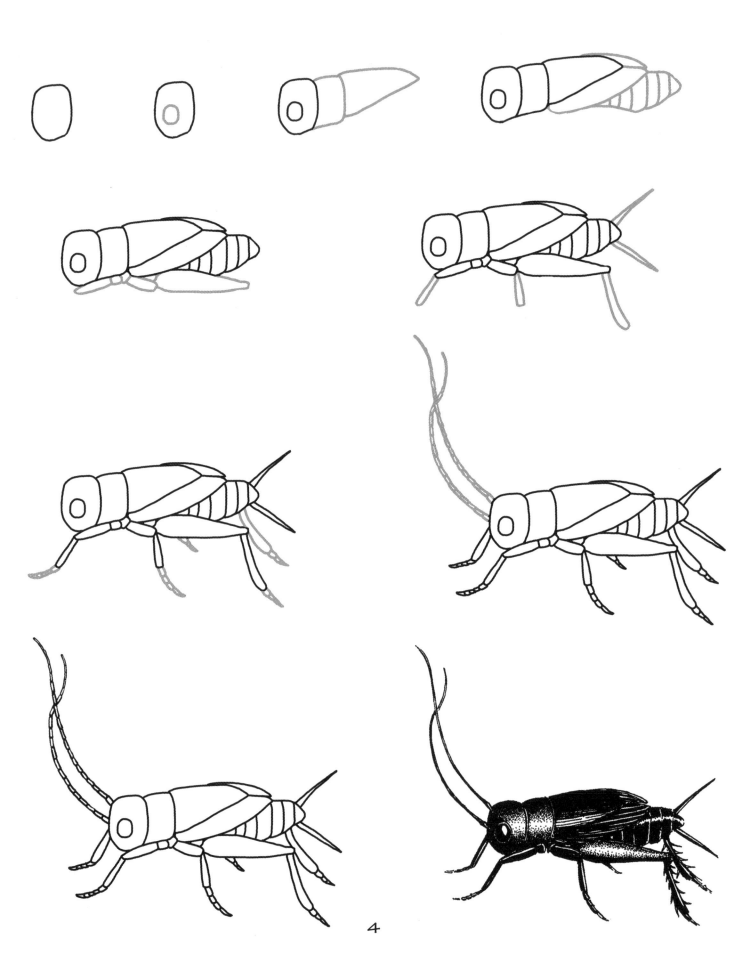

Draw a Dragonfly

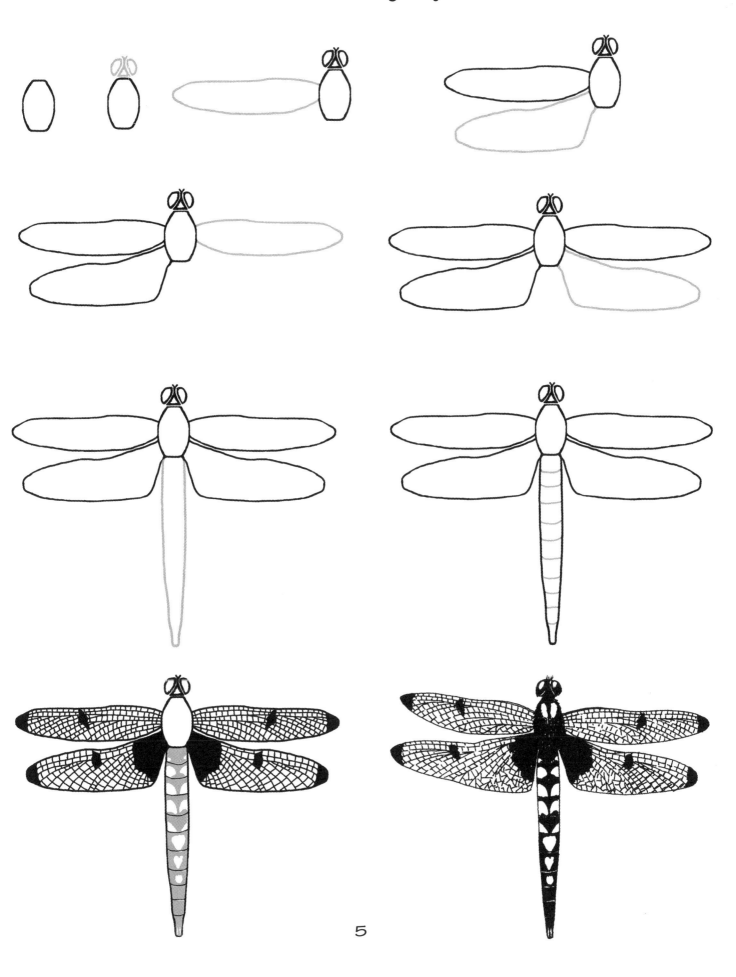

Draw a Grasshopper

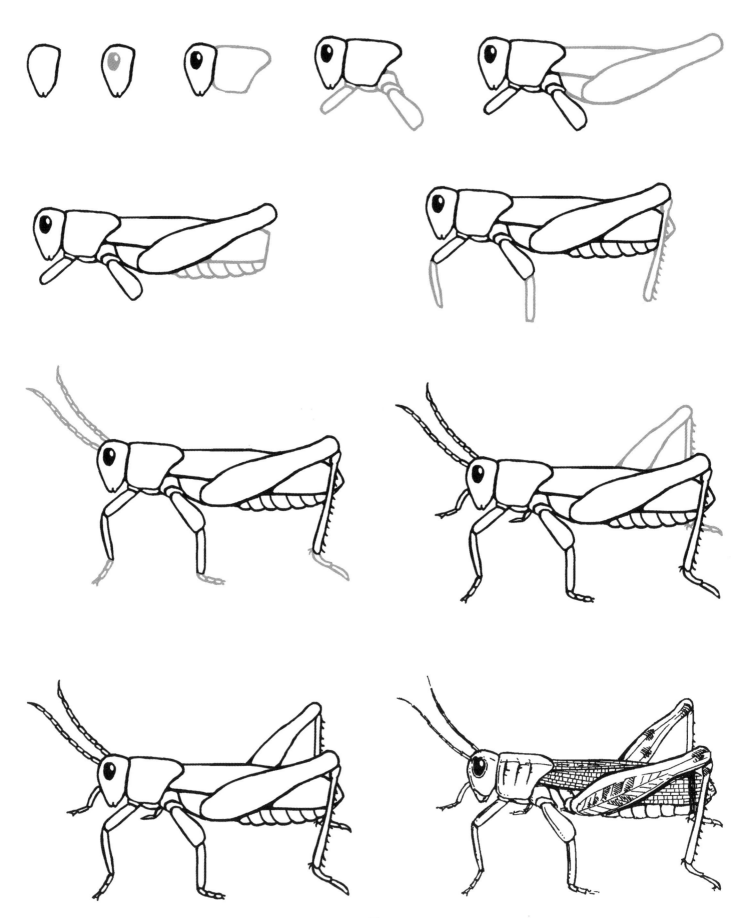

Draw a Honeybee

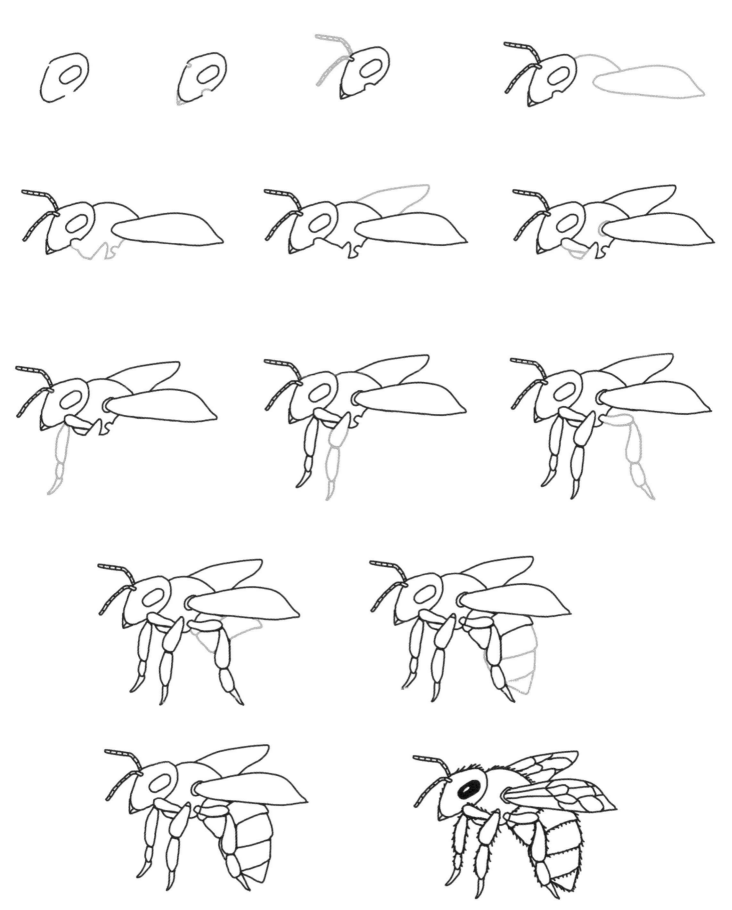

Draw a Ladybug Beetle

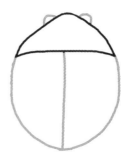
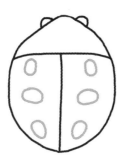

Draw a Swallowtail Butterfly

Spiders and Webs

Spiders are not insects, having eight legs and two body parts. This is a simple drawing of an argiope spider and a simple web. Start with a hexagon and draw four lines across the center to form the frame of the web.

Draw a Garden Spider

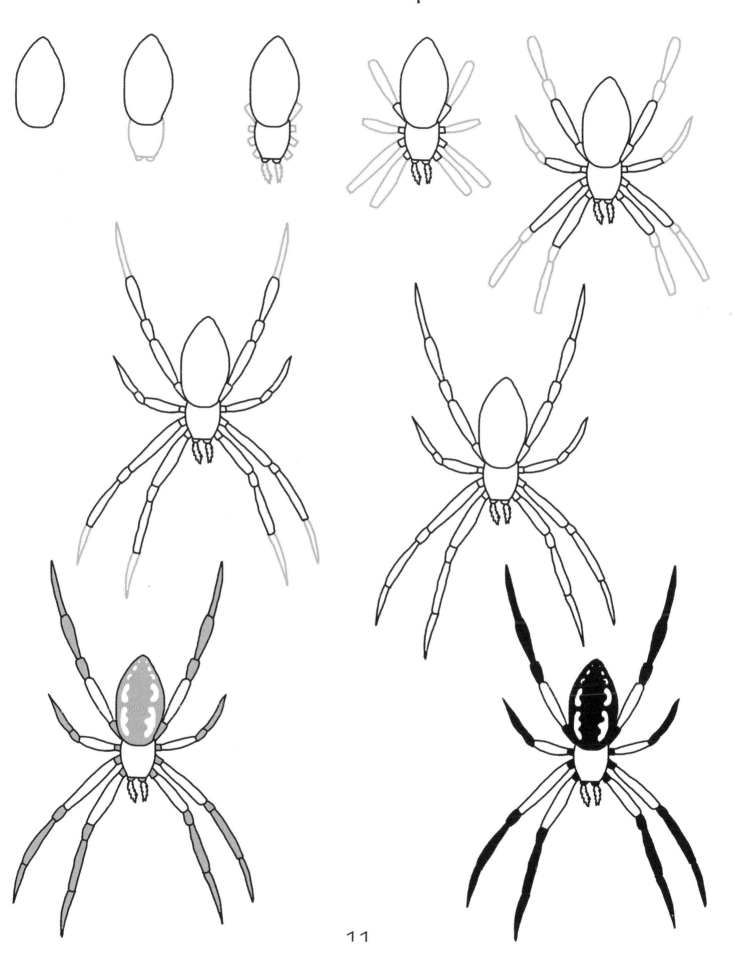

Drawing Birds

There are many different species of birds in the Adirondacks; each with their own distinct characteristics. For successful drawings look closely at the varying sizes and shapes of their heads, bodies, and beaks. Note also their movements and the way they hold their bodies when perching or standing. These different characteristics help identify the bird when seen in the wild. Understanding what makes each species of bird unique will help the artist bring them to life in their work.

Draw an American Goldfinch

Goldfinches are bright yellow with a white rump patch and a black forehead, wings and tail. The females and winter males are duller in color.

13

Draw a Black-capped Chickadee

The Chickadee, at 4-5" long, is a small, agile bird. Its head is black with a large white cheek patch — though sometimes it is described as white with a black cap and black bib. It is a seed, bug, and berry eater with a small, pointed beak. It moves very quickly and perches at all different angles. It tolerates cold temperatures well and feeds all winter. A feeder by the window will enable you to sketch its antics year round.

Draw a Canada Goose

The Canada Goose can be up to 25" tall with a long, black neck. It has a triangular-shaped beak and sloping head with a distinct white cheek patch. Its body is large in proportion to its long, slender neck. Like many waterfowl, they have bodies that are darker on top and lighter-colored underneath. They are often seen in large flocks grazing in fields or parks.

Draw a Cardinal

The Cardinal measures just under 8." It has a distinct head crest and a conical-shaped beak used for cracking seeds. The male is bright red in color while the female is more of a yellow-brown. Both have a dark face, but the male has a black area around the beak and eyes. Watch them at feeders in the spring, where you can sketch them while they feed.

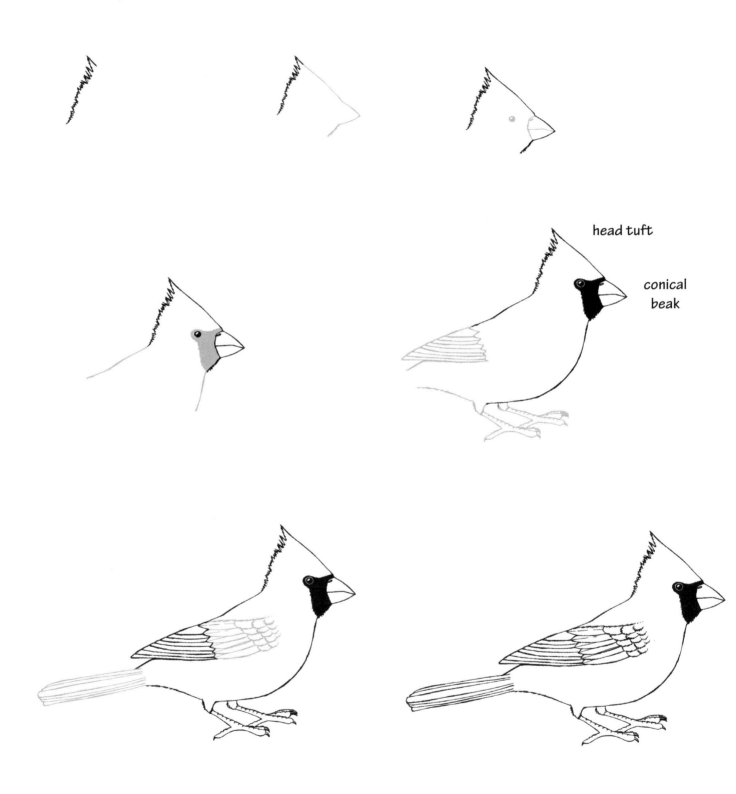

Draw a Common Merganser

The Common Merganser's head is sweeping like the loon but the bill is long, thin, and serrated with a hook on the end for catching fish. The white breast and sides help identify it. It is more slender in appearance than the loon.

Draw a Great Blue Heron

The Great Blue Heron is the tallest bird in the region standing over 4' tall. Its long curved neck and large beak are worth studying as it stands statue-like in the shallows on lakes, ponds, and streams. Drawing the neck well is a challenge but is necessary for a realistic portrayal of the heron. Also note the black wing patch, head crest, and chest fringe.

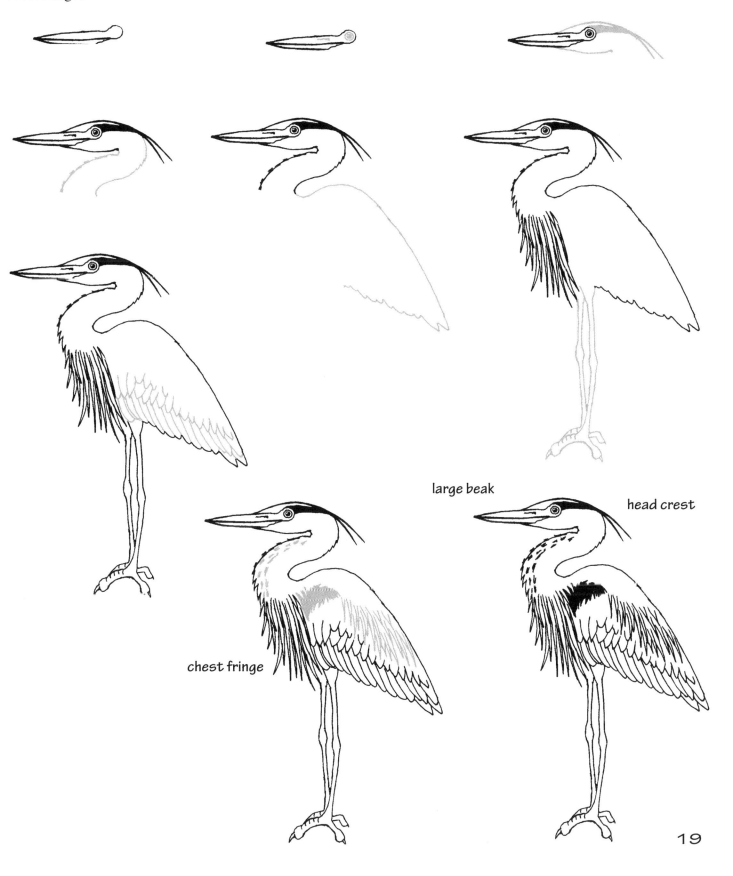

Draw a Great Horned Owl

At 20" tall, this owl is the largest in its range. Its "horns" are actually tufted ears. Active at night, owls are rarely seen except at dusk. A great horned owl can be identified by its flat, round face with eyes set forward for 3-D vision (adapted for its hunting style). When perched, its head and body is bulkier than a hawk's. The great horned owl's eyes are set under a distinct brow and framed on the sides by dark arcs. Its body is covered by horizontal bars.

Draw a Hairy Woodpecker

The Hairy Woodpecker is 8-9" tall and perches upright when pecking for insects. It has a white back and belly with black and white barred wings. Note the long, slender beak for pecking. It has a red patch on the back of its head. The downy woodpecker is identical but distinctly smaller in size.

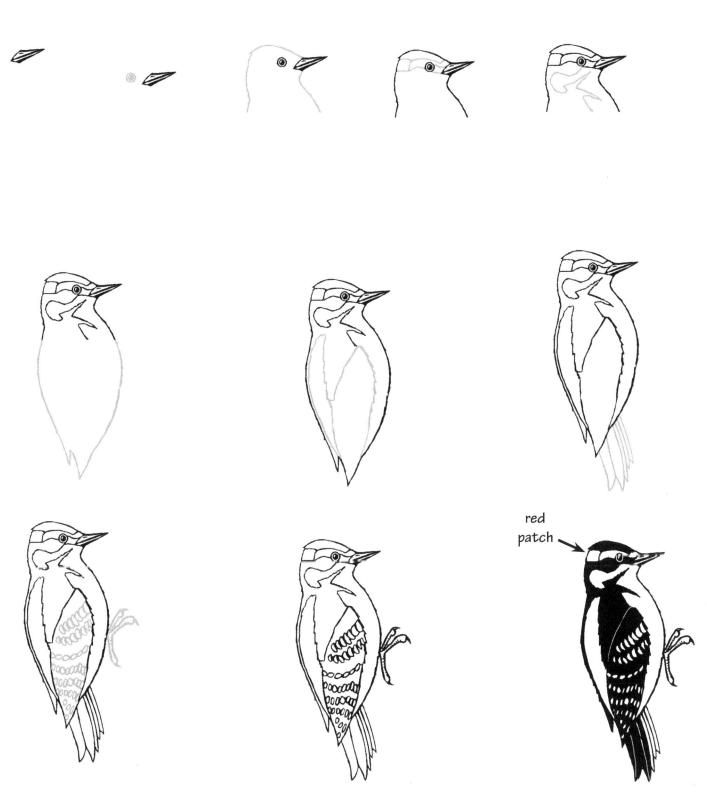

Draw a House Sparrow

The House Sparrow, 5-6", is common at feeders. Distinguish it from other sparrows by its dark neck and chest patch and its white cheek patch.

dark chest patch

Draw a Robin

The Robin is an 8.5" tall member of the thrush family, some of the larger song birds. The Robin has a dark back that is distinct against its even darker head. It has a reddish breast and white eye ring. It may be seen cocking its head while it hunts for worms, using its eyes to spot prey, as it does not have exceptional hearing or sense of smell. Robins have a very rounded breast and often take an upright stance with beaks pointed to the sky.

Note upright stance and large, rounded breast.

dark head and white eye ring

Draw a Ruby-throated Hummingbird

This Hummingbird is 3" tall and is the only one found in the northeastern U.S. Its flight is so rapid and agile (they can fly backwards!) that it is difficult to draw while observing them. Its long bill is adapted for collecting nectar from tubular flowers. Its feet are small and not made for walking (just to perch). It does not perch while feeding though, but hovers as illustrated here.

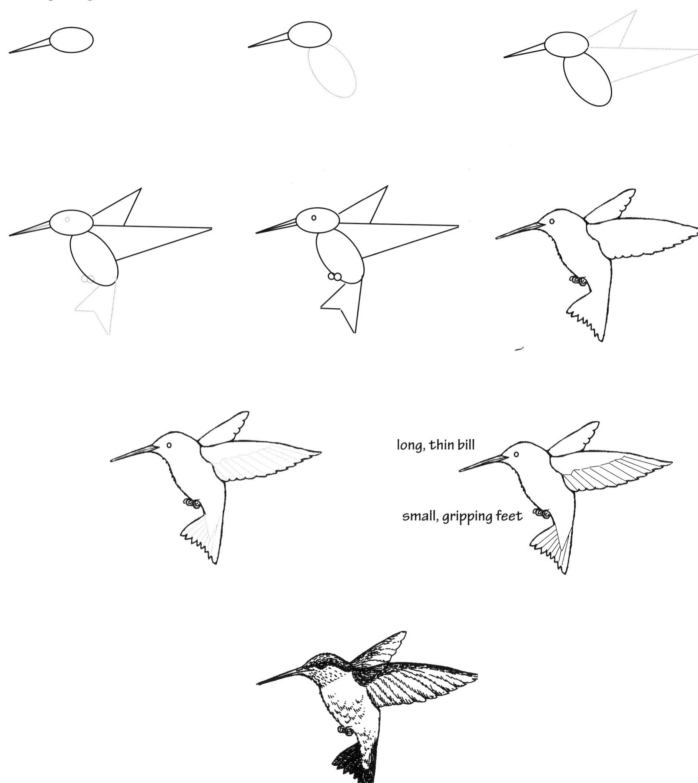

Draw a Tree Swallow

Tree Swallows have long, pointed wings and a notched tail, a green back and a white belly.

Drawing Mammals

There are many types of mammals, each group with its own distinctive body shape. Because all wild mammals are shy of humans and many are nocturnal, it may be hard to observe them first hand. It will be easier to practice drawing mammals from photographs, collecting as many pictures as you can to look at the animal from different angles. To draw a likeness it also helps to know in which group, or order, the mammal is classified. Even though each animal has separate and distinct characteristics, they do share physical similarities that place them in their particular group. The taxonomy of an eastern chipmunk would look like this:

Kingdom	-	Animal
Phylum	-	Vertebrate
Class	-	Mammal
Order	-	Rodentia
Family	-	Chipmunk
Genus	-	Tamias
Species	-	striatus

In the example below the deer mouse, squirrel, and chipmunk are all in the order *Rodentia*. Look at the similarities in their form. Now look at their differences. Drawing animals makes you really study how their bodies are put together. The taxonomy chart on the following pages gives the scientific description of mammals and how they are related.

- Mammal Taxonomy -
Mammal Orders

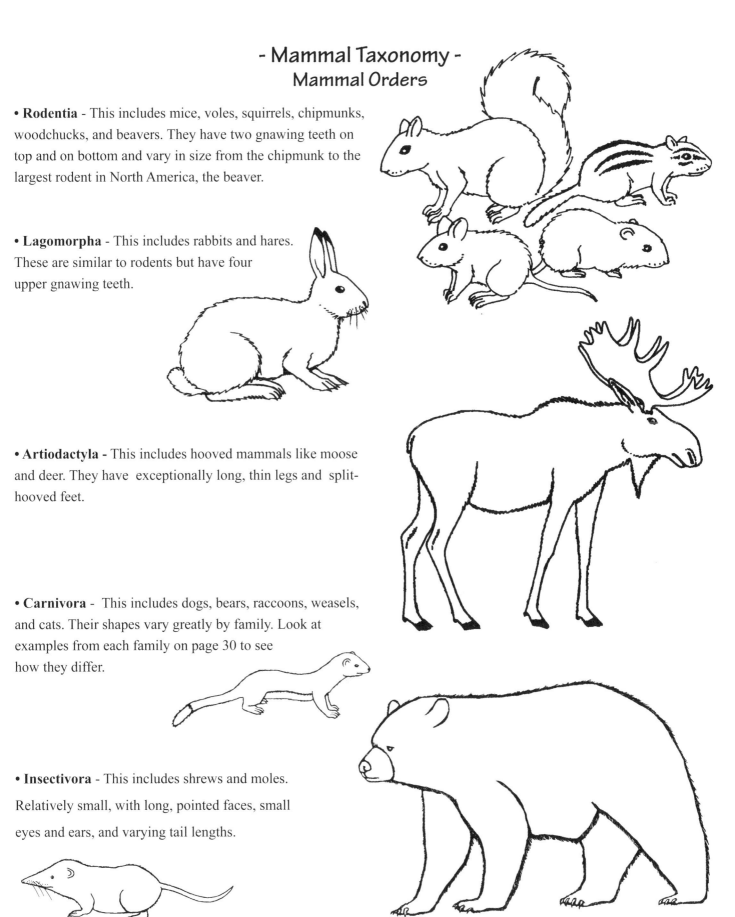

- **Rodentia** - This includes mice, voles, squirrels, chipmunks, woodchucks, and beavers. They have two gnawing teeth on top and on bottom and vary in size from the chipmunk to the largest rodent in North America, the beaver.

- **Lagomorpha** - This includes rabbits and hares. These are similar to rodents but have four upper gnawing teeth.

- **Artiodactyla** - This includes hooved mammals like moose and deer. They have exceptionally long, thin legs and split-hooved feet.

- **Carnivora** - This includes dogs, bears, raccoons, weasels, and cats. Their shapes vary greatly by family. Look at examples from each family on page 30 to see how they differ.

- **Insectivora** - This includes shrews and moles. Relatively small, with long, pointed faces, small eyes and ears, and varying tail lengths.

On the next page you can see how the order Carnivora is broken down into families.

Carnivore Families

- **Canidae** (dog family) includes wolves, coyote, and fox. They have a long snout, large, pointed ears, and long, bushy tail.

- **Felidae** (cat family) includes mountain lions, bobcats, and lynx. They have a short nose and in profile a short face. Their ears are smaller and rounder than a dog's.

- **Procyonidae** (raccoon family) raccoon only member here. They can vary greatly in size depending upon their food source.

- **Mustelidae** (scent gland family) includes weasels, skunks, and otters. They all have scent glands, but vary widely in body shape and form.

- **Ursidae** (bear family) black bear only member here. They have a rounded body with small rounded ears and short tail. They vary in color from tan to black.

Draw a Beaver

The beaver is the largest member of the rodent family in North America, weighing from 30-60 pounds. It has small eyes and ears relative to its body size. Its large, paddle-shaped tail has no fur on it. Its back feet are webbed.

Draw a Black Bear

The black bear is rarely seen as it is nocturnal and mostly solitary in its habits. It has small rounded ears and its nose is less furry than the rest of its body and often lighter in color. The black bear's body is bulky and rounded, with a short tail and muscular limbs.

Draw a Bobcat

Bobcats weigh up to 45 pounds. They have a light spotted coat with stripes on their short, stubby tail. They have smaller ear and cheek tufts than their relative, the lynx.

31

Draw a Coyote

The coyote looks like a medium-sized dog, with a pointier nose and a bushier tail. It is most often gray in color with a white or lighter throat and belly. It holds its tail down when running as opposed to the fox which holds its tail out.

Draw a Deer Mouse

The deer mouse has big eyes and ears for its small body size. Like many rodents it often sits on its haunches and holds food in its front paws to eat. It has a bicolored tail, dark on top and lighter underneath.

Draw a Deer

Male deer (stag) reach 200 pounds and grow spiked antlers that they shed in late fall and regrow every spring.

Draw an Eastern Chipmunk

The chipmunk's distinctive characteristics include facial stripes running across, above, and below the eye. Stripes also run down its sides and back. Its tail is not as bushy or large as the gray squirrel but is carried straight up when it runs.

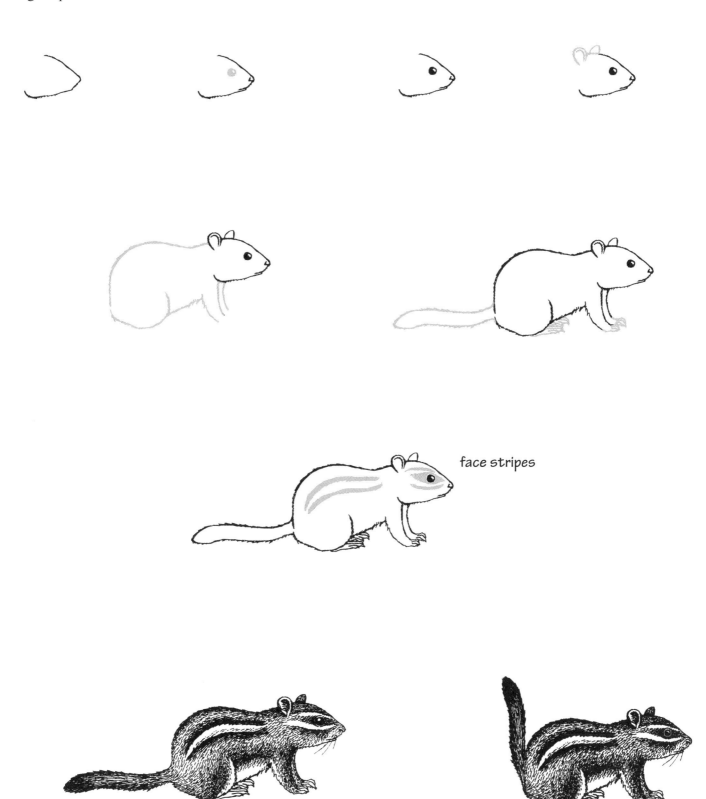

Draw a Flying Squirrel

The flying squirrel's body is dark above and lighter below with a loose fold of skin between the front and back legs that spreads for gliding. It has large eyes to suit nocturnal life.

Draw a Gray Squirrel

The gray squirrel has a bushy tail with white-tipped hairs around the border. It has large, rounded eyes and holds its tail up. It can be found in hardwood forests that contain nut trees.

Draw a Long-tailed Weasel

The long-tailed weasel is a long, thin, sleek mammal. The tail is about half the body length with a black tip. It turns white in the winter.

Draw a Meadow Vole

The meadow vole has a short tail. Its body is rounder than a mouse with small ears and eyes.

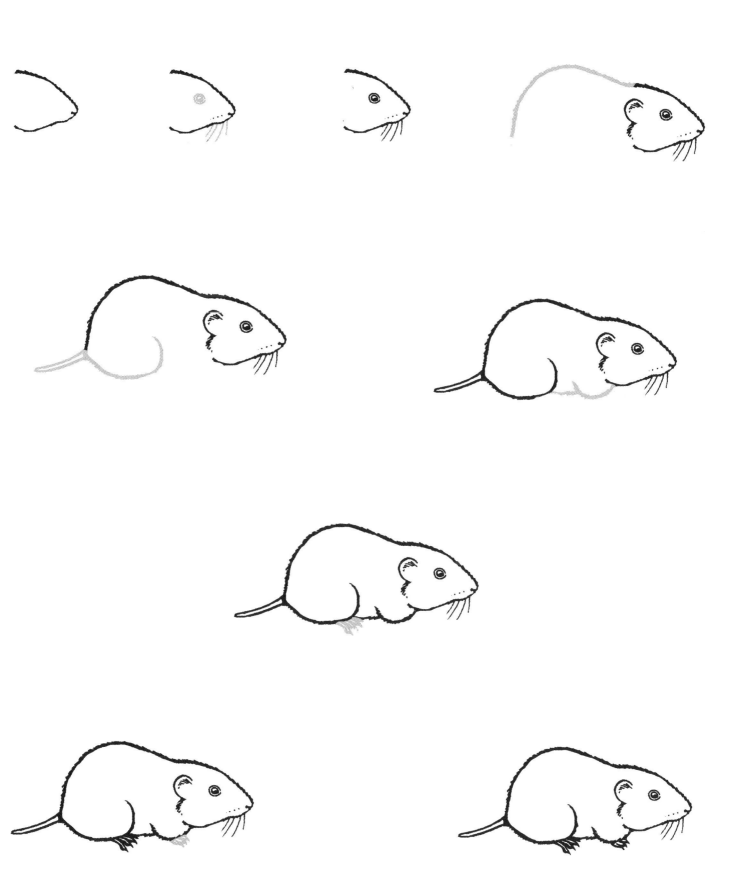

39

Draw a Moose

The moose is a very large mammal with adult males measuring 5 - 6.5' tall and weighing 850 - 1,180 pounds. It has a distinctive overhanging snout and a beard-like "bell" hanging off its throat. Its antlers are not like a deer's in that moose have a large, flat extension below the tips, often described as shaped like the palm of a hand with the antler tips extending like fingers. It has a hump over its shoulder area and its back slopes downward slightly from there. It has very long, spindly legs.

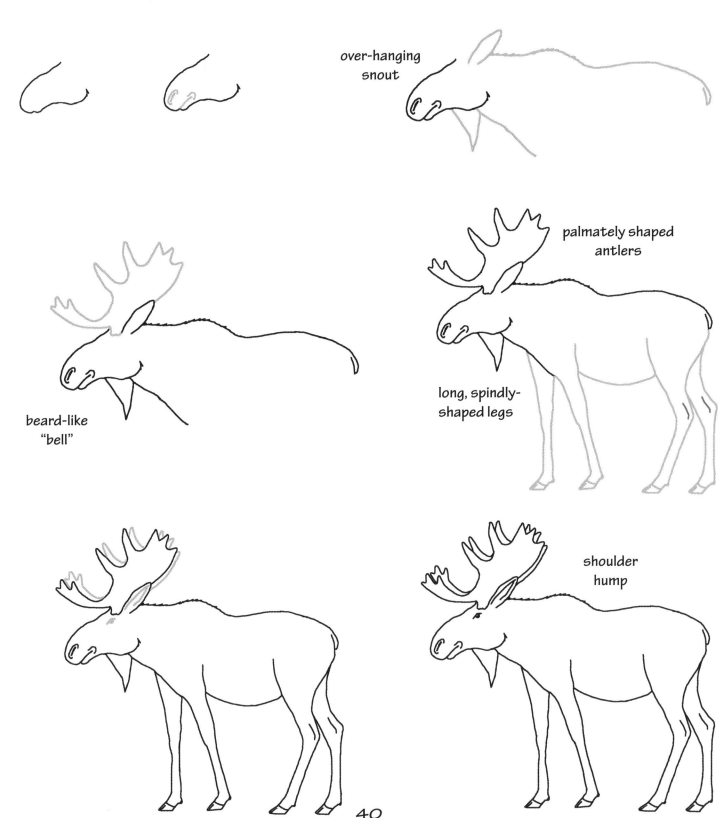

Draw a Mountain Lion

The mountain lion is the largest cat in North America, measuring 2.5 - 3' tall at the shoulder and up to 7' long from the nose to the tip of the tail. Yellow to gray in color, it has a black tip at the end of the tail. The backs of the ears are also dark colored.

Draw a Porcupine

The second largest of all rodents in the U.S., the porcupine has a small head, a large, rounded body and a long, thick, muscular tail. They can grow to 4 feet long including their tail and weigh up to 40 pounds. Their bodies are covered with stiff guard hairs and a band of sharp quills that runs down the center of the back (dorsally) from the head to the tip of the tail.

42

Draw a Raccoon

The raccoon is known for its black face mask and striped tail. Its back feet are longer than the small delicate front feet. Its body is rounded, not thin and sleek.

distinct white brow over eyes.

Draw a Red Fox

The red fox looks much like a small dog with reddish fur, a white belly, and a white-tipped bushy tail. The tail is red with black hairs mixed in and is carried held out when the fox travels. The legs and feet can be dark. Foxes can be seen during the day trotting across a field or road.

bushy tail

44

Draw a Shrew

The shrew family has some of the smallest mammals in the world. They have pointed faces with tiny eyes and ears. The masked shrew has a long tail.

Draw a Snowshoe Hare

The snowshoe hare's ears are relatively short compared to other hares at 3.5 - 4" long. It has large feet and turns white in winter. It is nocturnal and lives in forests and swamps.

large feet

Turns white in winter.

46

Draw a Woodchuck

The woodchuck has a rounded body with a bushy tail. It has small ears and eyes. It is the largest member of the squirrel family.

- Amphibians -
Draw a Bullfrog

The bullfrog is the largest frog in the Adirondacks at 4-8" long. It is green all over with darker green mottled areas. Its back legs are large and folded for leaping. It has protruding eyes and a visible tympani (eardrum).

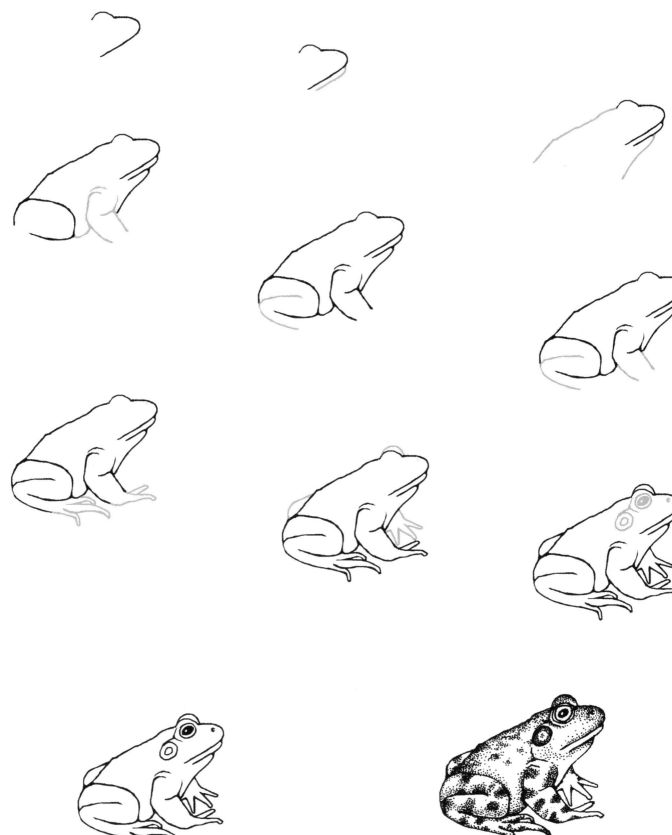

Draw a Red Eft (Newt)

Red efts are 2 - 4" long and orange to red in color with lighter spots.

Draw a Wood Frog

A wood frog is 2-3" long with a prominent dark mask around its eyes running to the tip of its nose and a white stripe along its upper "lip." Like all frogs, its back legs are large and folded for leaping. They have protruding eyes and a visible tympani (eardrum).

prominent eyes

white upper lip

large folded back legs

- Reptiles -
Draw a Snapping Turtle

The snapping turtle is the largest turtle in the Adirondacks, measuring from 8 - 18" long. It has a long spiked tail and a large rough shell often covered with algae.

- Fish -
Draw a Largemouth Bass

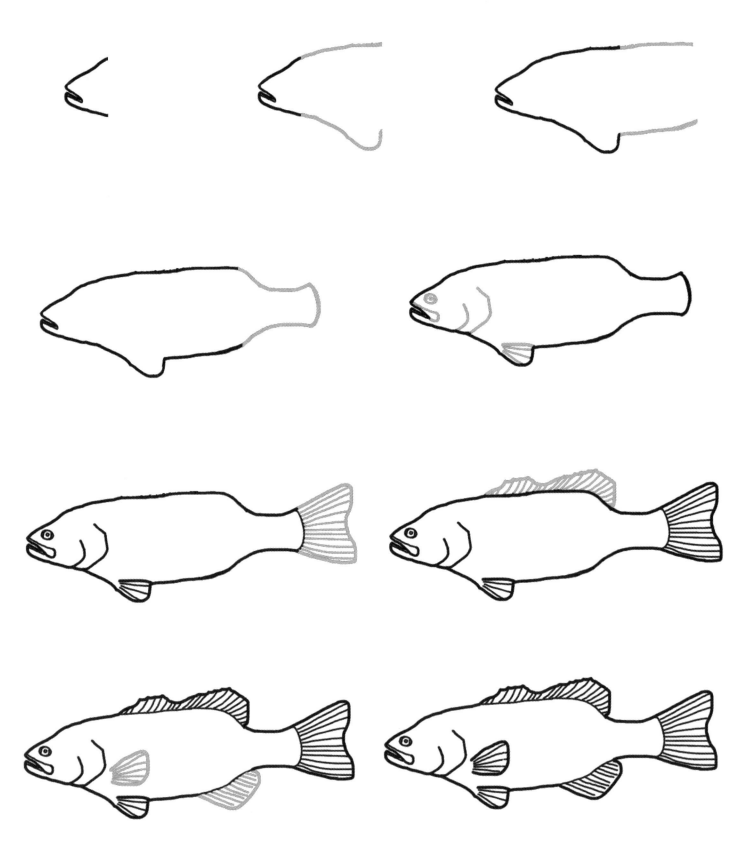

Draw a Trout

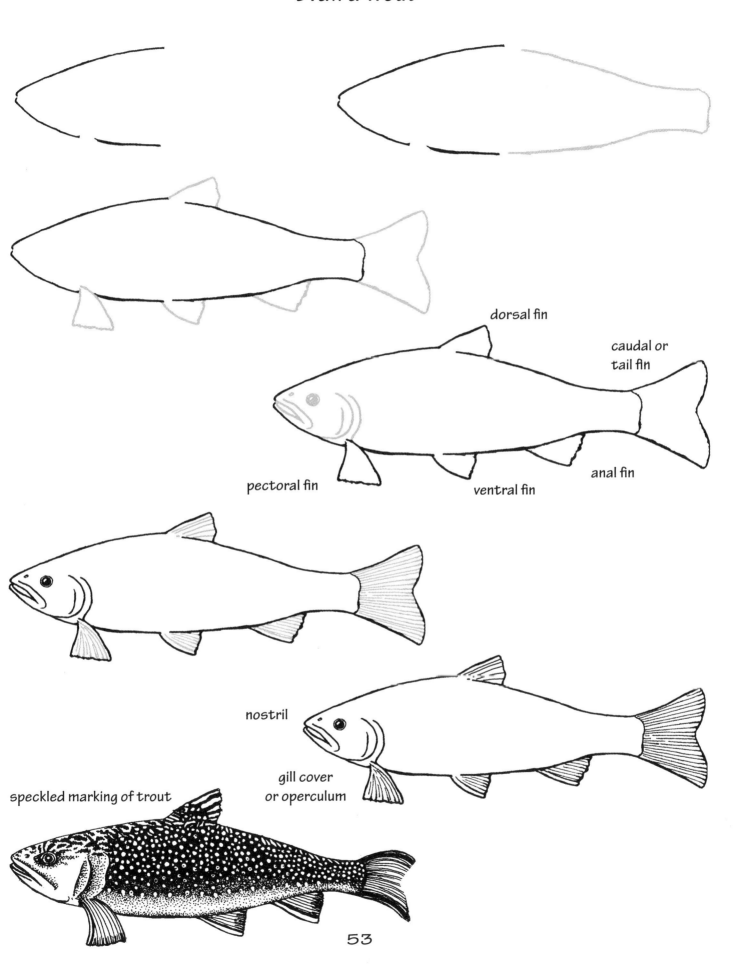

- Trees and Wildflowers -
Draw the Leaves

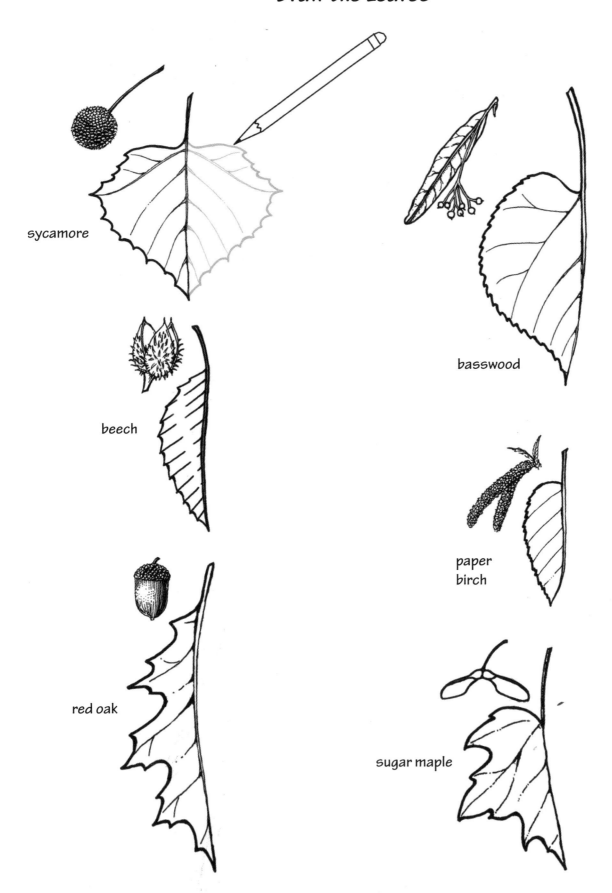

sycamore

basswood

beech

paper birch

red oak

sugar maple

Draw the Spring Wildflowers

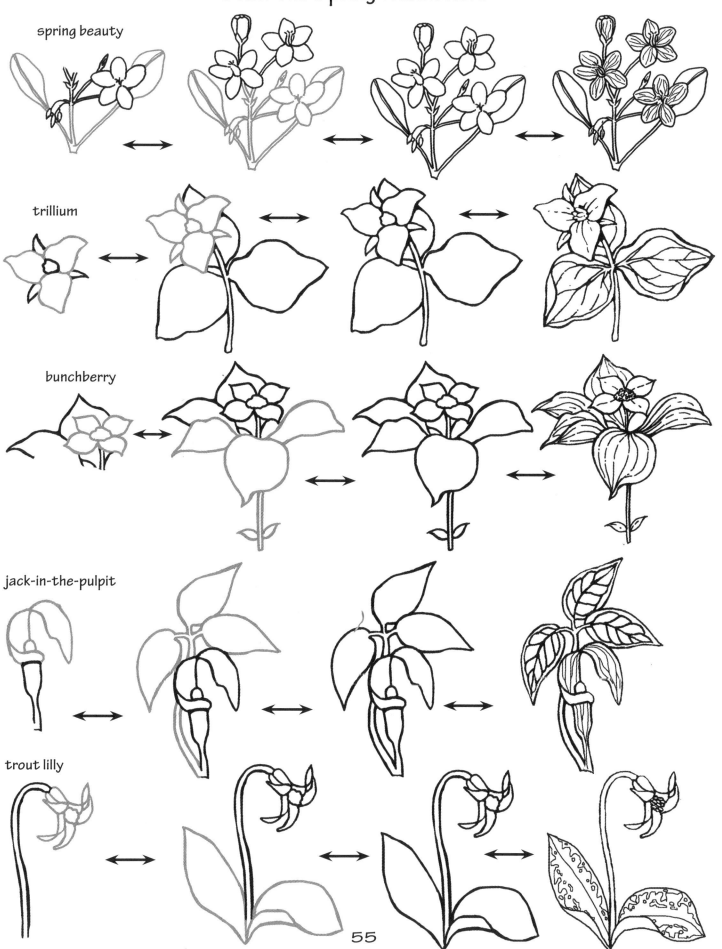

About the Author

Sheri Amsel has been writing and illustrating books for thirty years. Her life long interest in nature and the outdoors led to degrees in botany and zoology from the University of Montana, followed by a master's degree in anatomy and biomedical illustration from Colorado State University. During this time, Sheri took part in a summer internship at the Smithsonian Institute in Washington, D.C. in scientific illustration and published her thesis on the anatomy of the llama (illustrated, of course!). Her background has allowed her work to include writing and illustrating children's books and field guides, school and library workshops, outdoor education, nature trail development, and teaching college science. In 2009, Sheri was awarded the *Elizabeth Abernathy Hull Award for Outstanding Contributions to the Environmental Education of Youths*, by the Garden Club of America. Her latest project is **Exploringnature.org** – an comprehensive illustrated science resource website for students, educators and homeschool families. Sheri works out of her home studio in the Adirondack Mountains.